Struggling, Striving, Yet Always Smiling

Shreya Peshori

BookLeaf Publishing

India | USA | UK

Presentation by *BookLeaf Publishing*

Web: www.bookleafpub.com

E-mail: info@bookleafpub.com

ISBN: 978-93-5744-323-4

First edition 2022

DEDICATION

To my mother Neelu for giving me the positive encouragement I always need.

To my father Anil for building my self-confidence and motivation.

To my brother Samir for being my pillar of strength and inspiration.

To God for this life and my loved ones.

The sacrifices you make never go unnoticed. Thank you for lessening my fears and worries, and spoiling me with endless support and love.

Running Time

Hearing the wind chime ring
Seeing children on their phones
Hearing the birds sing
Seeing how we're even more alone

Where I used to run my feet in the grass
Spinning round and round
Reminiscing through a looking glass
Is the only way to feel less bound

A time when I spent more time within the trees
And less in front of a screen
Missing that feeling of being free
Amidst nature so serene

When life felt slow
I didn't need to know where to go
When life was free of worry
And was not so blurry

I would rewind if I had a clock
And savor the scenery on a walk

मिट्टी की खुशबू

हम नही जानते
की हम कितना खाते ।
किसान के काम
में है शोभा और नाम ।

लम्बे दिन और लम्बी रात
ज़मीन में है उनके हाथ ।
भारत की जान
है यह किसान की शान ।

प्यार से करते मेहनत
पर हम नही सोचते, है ना?
मिट्टी की खुशबू और उनके फल
किसान का त्याग और उनके हल

किसान नहीं तोह हम नहीं
हमारे लिए खाना नहीं
हमें मानना चाहिए उनका एहसान
देते है हमे भोजन का दान ।

कितने अच्छे है हमारे किसान
देश में वह सबसे महान ।

Optimistic Outlook

Having faith that there's an ocean
When you can only see a puddle
Believing your team can recover
When you're 3-nil down in your huddle

Hoping to receive an offer
After countless declines
Waiting patiently for your turn
When there's so many ahead in line

Working to perfect a solo when you can only
hum
Believing that what is meant for you will come

Knowing the sorrow you feel now
Is nothing compared to the joy and peace
coming
Knowing the fields you work to plough
Will provide you with harvests upcoming

Realizing that everyone wants happiness
And no one wants pain
But you can't have a rainbow
Without a little rain

My Only Regret

My only regret
Is not saying yes

Yes to the friends inviting me to their house
Yes to wearing the out-of-my-comfort-zone
blouse
Yes to going grocery shopping with my dad
Yes to listening to others when I get mad

Yes to planting flowers with my mom
Yes to going out after prom
Yes to taking a group photo
Yes to painting my own Van Gogh

Yes to writing down my thoughts
Yes to making up after I fought
Yes to the foreign guy looking to make a friend
Yes to reaching out and making amends

Yes to visiting my grandma in the nursing home
Yes to the urges to just roam
Yes to pausing my work to sit in the sun
Yes to being proud when I was done

Work isn't All

A seesaw, a gymnast's beam
A scale, a yin and yang
Balance is the name of the game
Yet humans give more and more time to make a
name

A medal, an honor
A trophy, a praise
Working beyond the given return and pay
Why do we base our worth on how productive
we are that day?

A cup, a gallon
A meter, a foot
Success is not a quantity, nor is it the end goal
It is a feeling, a state, that you should feel in
your soul

A house, a car
An income, a star
Others are not equals if they don't have such
But our work is still ever too much

The culture of hustle is an illness

Where people do not get to breathe and rest
Work is not life, it is only a part
Yet we are constantly tired and stressed

How much one works is not a competition, nor
race
Each person deserves rest and space
Hopefully we can be the ones to replace
Such a mindset and headspace

To the Beat

As my legs form a twirl,
my arms go out in a swirl.
As my eyes twinkle and gleam,
my lips curl with a beam.

My feet move without having to think
As the tune and rhythm vibrate in sync
Beautiful lyrics flutter and never seem to cease
And my mind is in a state of peace

My body conforms to the beat
Dancing is to me is a true treat
Where I can express my raw emotions
And time feels as if it's in slow motion

Where I can be imaginative and creative
Telling a story that's innovative
Creating and perfecting my own moves
Letting my thoughts glide and groove

An escape from reality and space
Churning out steps with balance and grace
As worries and stresses begin to melt
Conveying messages, celebrating lives heartfelt
Experimenting with boundless routines

A way of beauty and feeling like a queen

An outlet to find and lose myself
My heart races, a warm rush fills my body
If this is passion, may it last a lifetime

My Best Friends

The two that held my finger as I took a step
The two that kissed my head before I slept
The two that fed me before them
The two that captured my smiles and laughs
My parents are my best friends

The ones who have known me from day one
The ones who have seen me at my best and
worst
The ones who have sacrificed their joys for mine
The ones who have the answers to all my
problems
My parents are my best friends

Supporting me through every obstacle
Raising me to remain humble and sincere
Guiding me through every stage of life
Believing in me when I don't believe in myself
My parents are my best friends

Encouraging my passions and interests
Spoiling me with love and kindness
Instilling values, character, understanding
Acting as a pillar of strength and inspiration
My parents are best friends

Surviving sleepless nights, fulfilling constant
needs
Enduring cranky spells and bickering,
My parents have endlessly been there.

Likewise, I hope to be there for my two best
friends
Supporting the friends who have done so for me
Loving the two who have loved me for who I am

For the two best friends who have been there for
me
I promise to be there for them,
Forever and always.

The Beauty of Senses

The light through the curtain pours in
The sun's rays begin to tickle my skin
The layers and wrinkles in the bed are warm
I can hear Mother Nature brewing a storm

My feet hit the ground and tense
I can smell some slight mahogany incense
The water from the sink falls in a cold stream
I try to recall the last bits of my dream

I feel the smooth wood beneath
My tongue slides over my teeth
The aroma of ginger tea is strong
The blue jays are chirping their song

The sound of rain patters on the door
I chuckle at the squeak of the drawer
The shower fills the room with steam
The cozy warm water makes my body beam

I go outside to hear the trees rattle and bustle
The weekend is a rest from the busy hustle
The wind whispers in a sweet gentle tune
With such a sight, I realize my boon

I climb the fuzzy steps to quickly arrive
At the corner where I feel most alive
I remove my slippers to enter the room
Thanking God for my life & senses, despite the
outside gloom

Young, Wild, and Free

this very second will not return
it will never be noon on this very day ever again
nor will the sun shine in the exact same way

this very moment will not return
it will never be the perfect moment to do
something new
the moment must be made perfect

this very feeling will not return
you will never feel the weightlessness on your
shoulders again
nor have the freedom to let go and be

this very ability will not return
you will never be able to run and move freely
again
nor have the strength to carry on

this very youth will not return
you will never be able to heal, laugh, and make
mistakes like this
nor have the drive to go on adventures

this very wildness will not return
you will never forgive yourself for not being
more spontaneous
for going with the flow and seeing what happens

this very life will not return
you will never get second chances
regret invades persistently

make sure to live freely and fully

Salute to our Soldiers

To the women and men
That serve with dignity and pride
A cause larger than them and their stride

Waving high in the sky
With its patriotic hue,
Whether wet or dry, the fabric pulls through

They're hoisted up by their deeds
For their sacrifice for the nation
And our sincere appreciation

The pole is their loyalty
As strong as a wall that cannot be hurt
Nor tarnished with mounds of dirt

The stars and stripes are their bold, brilliant
uniforms
They stand up for what's right
In bright days or dull, gloomy nights

They represent our united nation
It takes bravery and courage,
Which others can only immensely encourage

To The Girl in the Mirror

to the girl in the mirror,
your scars don't define you
your crow's feet brighten you

your body hair isn't shameful
your hair is a mane that's graceful
your acne shouldn't be covered
your eyes would melt a lover

your brows are not bushy
your rosy cheeks are soft and mushy
your lips aren't cracked
your pain is limited to your lower back

your curves are a highlight
your scrunched nose as you laugh is a delight
your teeth are more than their hue
your fat is not more than the worth of you

your body is a temple
be more proud and gentle
your body is a temple
be more accepting and less judgmental

All the Boys Who Never Loved Me

it became difficult
to believe my own self love when I wasn't sure
that others can love me whole and pure

it became difficult
to not question my looks or traits
when boys never took me out on a date

it became difficult
to believe I was normal when boys never talked
to me
as they did to other girls while I would see

it became difficult
to believe my worth when I hadn't had my first
kiss
alas the loneliness I couldn't dismiss

it became difficult
to forget about love when romance was my
favorite movie theme
my unfulfilled desire, the one that would make
me dream

it became difficult
to see girls display their relationship and flaunt
their boyfriend online
when that was an unknown word in the world of
mine

it became difficult
to not think about love and to just eat and pray
but to hope and wish it would happen someday

it became easy
to cherish myself, realize nothing was wrong,
and develop self love
when I realized, over anything, that was most
above

एक नारी का स्वरूप

सुंदर साड़ी में एक नारी
उभर आती है।

लाल बिंदिया नैनों के बीच
उसका शृंगार बढ़ाती है।

मेहंदी उसके हाथों को सजाती है।
काजल उसके आँखों को निखारती है।

उसकी पायल पैरों में
खनखनाती है।

चूड़ियाँ उसकी कलाइयों में
छनछनाती है।

उसकी अदा में एक शक्ति है
जो परिवार बनाती है।

और क्या मैं कहूँ ......
इस नारी के स्वरूप को,
जो यह संसार रचाती है।

The Best Stage

When waking up felt like a breeze
When work was completed with ease
When the day began with soccer and bike rides
When the day ended with park swings and slides
When the biggest worry was who controlled the
tv remote
When class would consist of passing notes

When a normal day meant bickering with my
brother
When the world felt better by hugging my
mother
When Mario Kart and Pokémon were my
pastimes
When I became used to the sound of a wind
chime

When climbing a tree was a goal
When spinning in circles warmed my soul
When creating games to play was the norm
When my joy exploded when we had a
snowstorm

When blowing bubbles gave me a thrill
When my dresses had polka dots and frill

When seeing bunnies was the highlight of my
day
When I would run through sprinklers and feel
their spray

When I would be truly me and never be shy
When I would appreciate the clouds in the sky
When I only took two days to read a book
When I never cared about how I looked

When I would ask endless questions about life
When I didn't know the meaning of strife
When I spent more time outdoors and nature
was at its peak
When the world felt beautiful and felt unique

The best stage of my life was my childhood
When stress didn't exist, and I would only find
good

Speed of Advancement

How fast has it been
From Ford's assembly line
To electric vehicles and space travel

How fast has it been
From flip and sliding phones
To ones with touch screens

How fast has it been
From developing a camera's film
To taking and editing countless clicks

How fast has it been
From reading maps and signs
To machines that tell us when to turn right

How fast has it been
From papers and pens
To typing notes and accessing them anywhere

How fast has it been
From long distance calls
To global video calling for free

How fast has it been

From shopping in stores
To receiving things straight from home

How fast has it been
From landscapes and trees
To building more houses and condo scenes

How fast has it been
From seeing the stars at night
To soon seeing the end of earth's time

Technology and advancement is constant
Change is rapid, inevitable
Yet we must question and evaluate the change
If it takes us farther away from our surroundings
and senses
Or if it brings us closer to our detriment and end

The Thief of my Life

If someone can, please catch the thief of my life
He has taken my innocence and light
I used to be secure in my work and myself
However, he's convinced me I'm no longer
bright

The thief stole more from me as I became older
He sparks my anxiety and ignites worry inside
Made me question my purpose and worth
And injects comments that are degrading and
snide

The thief is subtle, committing crime without
notice
He makes my accomplishments seem small and
weak
His online presence is most pronounced
He highlights my shortcomings, making me feel
bleak

In a world so big, he makes me focus on
miniscule details
Cements my worry that no matter how hard I try
It will never be enough and that I'll never

Reach there, so might as well just cry

He's made me desire for other people's lives
Wishing I could be them, or have what I lack
Hoping to look like them, achieve what they
have
A blow to my confidence, my happiness
attacked

It's taken a while, but I caught the thief of my
life
Who made me believe I was inadequate and
behind
Comparison has done nothing but steal my joy
Thus the key to his capture was...changing my
frame of mind

An Attitude of Gratitude

It's sad to think some people are never fulfilled
That they never feel happy in their place
They never feel satisfied
Since they get caught in the race

They don't realize their present blessings
Aiming to do better, achieve more and more
Not appreciating their current life
Not being thankful for what they have in store

Happiness and satisfaction feels far away
When humans just focus on what they lack
When they are not grateful for each day and
When they only look at the drawbacks

Being present in the moment
Being thankful for the little things
Hopefully they will learn
What this attitude helps to bring

Rejecting the "happiness" of material items
A sense of relief, a sense of joy
Taking in nature, laughing with loved ones
That is the true blessing to enjoy

Happiness is not obtained
When people reach every milestone
It is a sense of realizing every sunshine
And every storm you have been thrown

Acknowledging all that you've been given,
And taking in how much you've grown

Take The Path Less Traveled, But Don't Get Lost

society tells us to stay on the path,
but I wanted to take an undiscovered road.

society tells us to choose a typical career,
but my heart did not feel right.

society tells us to not experiment,
but I was tempted to combine new ingredients
together.

society tells us to follow the crowd,
but I always felt overwhelmed by so many
people.

society tells us to have a plan,
but I for once wanted to be spontaneous.

society tells us to look straight,
but I felt happy roaming in the scenery around.

society tells us to be quiet,
but I wanted to create noise and chaos.

society tells us to sit still,

but I naturally began to dance around.

If I had listened to society,
I would have been miserable and bitter.
If I had listened to society,
I would be upset with myself.

society told me to walk,
but they don't know I had an urge to fly,
and fly I did.

Curiosity Saved the Cat

If people hadn't been curious,
Innovation would be an unfamiliar word
I'm not exactly a fan of technology and
engineering
Yet regardless I want my questions to be heard

How do cars work? How can planes fly?
Who created the Internet and why?

What makes stock prices go up and down?
Why does it take more muscles to frown?

How is perfume made? How are clothes sewn?
Where does trash go once it's thrown?

How are vaccines created? Who controls the
supply chain?
How does detergent remove tough stains?

Perhaps I want to know the mechanisms behind
most things
Like what makes trees keep their leaves once it
becomes spring?

Many only expect kids to be so curious

However, my questions rage like fast and furious
If a monkey named George can be inquisitive,
why can't I?
Sorry I want to know the who, what, where, and
why!

Gender Rules?

At age three, it began with soccer lessons
At age ten, it progressed with shoveling snow
At age thirteen, it advanced with mowing the
lawn
At age sixteen, it continued with lifting weights
At age nineteen, it heightened with investing in
the market

There was no time or place my parents
Treated their son differently than their daughter
In fact, I never realized myself until
A family friend commented that I offered
To help with some manual labor

I dressed like a tomboy in middle school
And my parents in fact were happy
To give me my brother's hand-me-downs
And I was blissful to have that freedom

I played coed soccer from elementary school
And continued all the way to university
Where my dad only encouraged me to
Not be afraid of shoving boys' shoulders

The kitchen was a place for both genders

Since such activities are life skills
Not gender-specific tasks
The yard was a work ground for both genders
Since the grass or leaves don't mind who tends
to them

Girls are no less, boys are no more
Those stereotypes should not exist anymore
Each family should treat both the same
Tasks and skills don't look at the person's name

Struggle is Survival

As long as there is life
There is struggle
As long as we can breathe
There are many things we must juggle

There are no highs if there aren't any lows
A roller coaster fanatic knows how this goes

Without bad times, we wouldn't savor good days
Without hard work, we wouldn't appreciate play

There is no one who hasn't faced sorrow and
grief
No tree that hasn't lost some sort of leaf

As long as there is life,
We must remain brave and strong
As long as we can breathe,
We must fight on.

Difficulties do not merely disappear
They are at every turn, every stage
The book of life will continue to go on
With beauty and pain on every page

If we waited for life to be easy
Before we decide to be cheerful
We would never be able to live fully
And we would always remain tearful

The true meaning of struggle is to
Maintain happiness and hope throughout
To realize each struggle too shall pass
Despite any stress or any doubt

We should enjoy our journey
And savor each and every second
Hardships will always be present
But we shouldn't sacrifice our joy, I reckon

Thus I may be struggling
I may be striving
Yet I promise you
I will always be smiling.